CW00385708

SPANISH KEY WORDS

The basic 2,000-word vocabulary
arranged by frequency in a
hundred units.

With comprehensive Spanish and
English indexes.

PEDRO CASAL

The Oleander Press

The Oleander Press
16 Orchard Street
Cambridge
CB1 1JT
www.oleanderpress.com

Revised & Updated 2017
© 1993 The Oleander Press
All Rights Reserved

ISBN: 9780906672266

Cover Photograph by
Enrique Dans

CONTENTS

Introduction

Spanish Key Words provides an easy route to mastering excellent basic Spanish. The 100-unit structure provides you with the most useful words quickly and easily, each unit consisting of 20 common words. These are the essential foundation stones on which you intuitively build your language framework. Computer analysis of a corpus of a million words has provided this essential list of the commonest two thousand key words in Spanish, with their meanings in English, arranged in decreasing order of frequency.

The first five units (100 words) account for 50% of conversational Spanish; the first 500 words account for 75% of normal usage; the full 2,000 will equip you for nearly all word occurrences of modern Spanish usage in speech, newspapers, books, television, internet etc. It also provides an all-in-one basic Spanish-English dictionary and an all-in-one basic English-Spanish dictionary.

Spanish Key Words is the perfect fast, easy aid to learning Spanish by using the simplest, most logical way to pick up a vocabulary of ten thousand words from just two thousand.

The Units

Each of the hundred units is self-contained, Unit 1 including the twenty commonest key words, Unit 2 the next commonest and so on. The key word is followed by an indication of its part of speech: *adj.*, adjective; *adv.*, adverb; *conj.*, conjunction, *f.n.*, feminine noun; *interj.*, interjection; *m.n.*, masculine noun; *num.*, numeral; *prep.*, preposition; *pron.*, pronoun. Verbs are not so shown, because they are represented in each instance by their infinitive, which is always translated beginning with 'to'.

Masculine nouns and adjectives form their feminine by changing their final vowel from *o* to *a*, unless otherwise shown. So masculine *amarillo* becomes feminine *amarilla*.

Singular nouns and adjectives form their plural by adding *s* if ending in a vowel, or *es* if ending in a consonant, unless otherwise shown. So singular *amarillo* becomes plural *amarillos* and singular *amarilla* becomes *amarillas*. So singular *lugar* becomes plural *lugares*.

Regular verbs ending in *ar*, *-er* and *-ir* are conjugated in model form in a separate table just before the hundred units. The commonest irregular verbs are conjugated (with pronouns and meanings in the early units) in the present tense of the active voice, indicative mood, wherever their infinitive occurs in order of frequency. Though verbs appear only in their infinitive form, their position in the units has been calculated from the total occurrence of all their parts.

Many Spanish words may be translated by a number of English equivalents. It would be counter-productive, in a work designed to stimulate interest rather than to clog the memory, to list all such equivalents, so only the most common have been cited, with the commonest of all first. When consulting the two indexes, therefore, the reader who cannot find a given word should try to think of synonyms or near-synonyms if a certain word seems to be omitted.

Regular Verbs
in the Present Tense

First Conjugation   Cantar,   to sing

yo canto	I sing	nosotros cantamos	we sing
tú cantas	you (s.) sing	vosotros cantais	you (pl.) sing
él canta	he sings	ellos cantan	they sing

Second Conjugation   Temer,   to fear

yo temo	I fear	nosotros tememos	we fear
tú tomes	you (s.) fear	vosotros teméis	you (pl.) fear
él teme	he fears	ellos temen	they fear

Third Conjugation   Partir,   to leave, depart

yo parto	I leave	nosotros partimos	we leave
tú partes	you (s.) leave	vosotros partis	you (pl.) leave
él parte	he leaves	ellos parten	they leave

N .B. Conventionally, 'él', 'he' stands also for 'ella', 'she' in the conjugation of the present tense throughout this frequency list.

SPANISH
KEYWORDS

Unit 1

de *(prep.)*	of
el *(m., pl. los - art.)*	the
la *(f. pl. las - art.)*	the
y *(conj.)*	and
a *(prep.)*	to, at
en *(prep.)*	in, into
él *(pron.)*	he
ser	to be, being

    yo soy   I am   nosotros somos   we are
    tú eres   you *(s.)* are   vosotros sois   you *(pl.)* are
    él es   he is   ellos son   they are

que *(pron.)*	that, which, who, what
haber	to have

    yo he   I have   nosotros habemos   we have
    tú has   you *(s.)* have   vosotros habéis   you *(pl.)* have
    él ha   he has   ellos han   they have

que *(conj.)*	that
su *(adj.)*	his, hers, its, your, their
no *(adv.)*	not
un *(m. - art.)*	a, an
por *(prep.)*	by, through
con *(prep.)*	with
una *(f. - art.)*	a, an
yo *(pron.)*	I
estar	to be

    yo estoy   I am   nosotros estamos   we are
    tú estás   you *(s.)* are   vosotros estáis   you *(pl.)* are
    él está   he is   ellos están   they are

tener	to have

    yo tengo   I have   nosotros tenemos   we have
    tú tienes   you *(s.)* have   vosotros tenéis   you *(pl.)* have
    él tiene   he has   ellos tienen   they have

Unit 2

ella *(pron.)*	she
para *(prep.)*	for
este *(adj.)*	this
lo *(art.)*	it
más *(adv.)*	more
como *(conj.)*	as, how
ello *(pron.)*	it
ir	to go

yo voy I go	nosotros vamos we go
tú vas you *(s.)* go	vosotros vais you *(pl.)* go
él va he goes	ellos van they go

decir	to say

yo digo I say	nosotros decimos we say
tú dices you *(s.)* say	vosotros decís you *(pl.)* say
él dice he says	ellos dicen they say

todo *(adj.)*	all, every, whole
tú *(pron.)*	you *(s., informal)*
pero *(conj.)*	but, yet
hacer	to do, make

yo hago I do	nosotros hacemos we make
tú haces you *(s.)* do	vosotros hacéis you *(pl.)* make
él hace he does	ellos hacen they make

poder	to be able

yo puedo I can	nosotros podemos we can
tú puedes you *(s.)* can	vosotros podéis you *(pl.)* can
él puede he can	ellos pueden they can

usted *(pron.)*	you *(s. formal)*
o *(conj.)*	either, or
ya *(adv.)*	already
otro *(adj.)*	another, other
mi *(adj.)*	my

Unit 3

ver	to see
yo veo	nosotros vemos
tú ves	vosotros veis
él ve	ellos ven
dar	to give
yo doy	nosotros damos
tú das	vosotros dais
él da	ellos dan
sin *(prep.)*	without
ese *(adj.)*	that
querer	to want
yo quiero	nosotros queremos
tú quieres	vosotros queréis
él quiere	ellos quieren
dos *(num.)*	two
hombre *(m.n.)*	man
nuestro *(adj.)*	our, ours
sobre *(pron.)*	on, above, about
porque *(conj.)*	because
cuándo *(adv.)*	when
mismo *(adj.)*	same
grande *(adj.)*	large, great
muy *(adv.)*	very
vida *(f.n.)*	life
vez *(f.n.)*	time, occassion
saber	to know
yo sé	nosotros sabemos
tú sabes	vosotros sabéis
él sabe	ellos saben
eso *(pron.)*	that
primer *(adj.)*	first
aquel *(adj.)*	that

Unit 4

entre *(prep.)*	between, among
día *(m.n.)*	day
don *(m.n.)*	Mr
sí *(adv.)*	yes
tan *(adv.)*	so
todo *(pron.)*	all, everything
también *(adv.)*	too, also
pues *(conj.)*	well, then
hasta *(pron.)*	until
algún *(adj.)*	any, some
año *(m.n.)*	year
aquí *(adv.)*	here
ni *(conj.)*	neither, nor
uno *(num.)*	one
pasar	to pass
venir	to come
yo vengo	nosotros venimos
tú vienes	vosotros venís
él viene	ellos vienen
señor *(m.n.)*	Mr, gentleman
cómo *(adv.)*	how? Why?
mujer *(f.n.)*	woman, wife
llegar	to arrive

Unit 5

creer	to believe
bien *(adv.)*	well
siempre *(adv.)*	always
mucho *(adj.)*	a lot of, much
casa *(f.n.)*	house
parecer	to seem
yo parezco	nosotros parecemos
tú pareces	vosotros parecéis
él parece	ellos parecen
ahora *(adv.)*	now
cosa *(f.n.)*	thing
hablar	to speak
deber	to have to, owe
dejar	to leave
así *(adv.)*	thus, so
dónde *(adv.)*	where?
tiempo *(m.n.)*	time
sólo *(adv.)*	only
tres *(num.)*	three
desde *(prep.)*	from, since
bueno *(adj.)*	good
parte *(f.n.)*	part
esto *(pron.)*	this

Unit 6

llevar	to bear, carry
mil *(adj. Num.)*	thousand
ciento *(adj. Num.)*	hundred
después *(adv.)*	afterwards
mundo *(m.n.)*	world
llamar	to knock, call (llamarse, to be called)
sino *(conj.)*	except, but (after negative)
poner	to put
yo pongo	nosotros ponemos
tú pones	vosotros ponéis
él pone	ellos ponen
vivir	to live
cual *(pron.)*	which, who, whom
obra *(f.n.)*	work
quedar	to remain
español *(adj.)*	Spanish
encontrar	to meet
pensar	to think
salir	to go out, leave
yo salgo	nosotros salimos
tú sales	vosotros salís
él sale	ellos salen
volver	to return
yo vuelvo	nosotros volvemos
tú vuelves	vosotros volvéis
él vuelve	ellos vuelven
pueblo *(m.n.)*	people, village
nuevo *(adj.)*	new
cada *(adj.)*	each

seguir	to follow
yo sigo	nosotros seguimos
tú sigues	vosotros seguís
él sigue	ellos siguen
quien *(pron.)*	who
antes *(adv.)*	before
conocer	to be acquainted with
yo conozco	nosotros conocemos
tú conoces	vosotros conocéis
él conoce	ellos conocen
aun *(adv.)*	even
tu *(adj.)*	your
mirar	to look at
verdad *(f.n.)*	truth
poco *(adj.)*	little, slight
tal *(adj.)*	such
señora *(f.n.)*	Mrs, lady
ciudad *(f.n.)*	city
oír	to hear, listen to
yo oigo	nosotros oímos
tú oyes	vosotros oís
él oye	ellos oyen
mano *(f.n.)*	hand
éste *(pron.)*	this
dios *(m.n.)*	god
hoy *(adv.)*	today
hora *(f.n.)*	hour
libro *(m.n.)*	book
historia *(f.n.)*	history

Unit 8

sentir	to feel, be sorry, hear
yo siento	nosotros sentimos
tú sientes	vosotros sentís
él siente	ellos sienten
ojo *(m.n.)*	eye
momento *(m.n.)*	moment
cierto *(adj.)*	certain, correct
menos *(adv.)*	less
cinco *(num.)*	five
palabra *(f.n.)*	word
caso *(m.n.)*	case, notice
nada *(pron.)*	nothing
siglo *(m.n.)*	century
hijo *(m.n.)*	son
último *(adj)*	last
padre *(m.n.)*	father
noche *(f.n.)*	night
casi *(adv.)*	nearly
idea *(f.n.)*	idea
punto *(m.n.)*	point
entrar	to enter
nunca *(adv.)*	never
entonces *(adv.)*	then

Unit 9

tanto *(adj.)*	so much, so many
tomar	to take
estado *(m.n.)*	state
décimo *(adj.)*	tenth
modo *(m.n.)*	way, method
escribir	to write
cuanto *(adj.)*	how much, how many
mucho *(adv.)*	a great deal, much
acabar	to have just, finish, end
luz *(f.n.)*	light
uno *(pron.)*	one
trabajo *(m.n.)*	work
luego *(adv.)*	then, later, next
tierra *(f.n.)*	land, earth
nombre *(m.n.)*	name
mayor *(adj.)*	greater, major, elder, oldest
calle *(f.n.)*	street
nadie *(pron.)*	nobody
aunque *(conj.)*	though, although
fin *(m.n.)*	end

Unit 10

amor *(m.n.)*	love
propio *(adj.)*	own
autor *(m.n.)*	author
ése *(pron.)*	that (one)
nada *(adv.)*	in no way
país *(m.n.)*	country
cuatro *(num.)*	four
esperar	to wait, hope, expect
otro *(pron.)*	other, another
madre *(f.n.)*	mother
amigo *(m.n.)*	friend
espíritu *(m.n.)*	spirit
grupo *(m.n.)*	group
ciencia *(f.n.)*	science
aparecer	to appear, seem
yo aparezco	nosotros aparecemos
tú apareces	vosotros aparecéis
él aparece	ellos aparecen
contar	to count, tell
yo cuento	nosotros contamos
tú cuentas	vosotros contáis
él cuenta	ellos cuentan
servir	to serve
yo sirvo	nosotros servimos
tú sirves	vosotros servís
él sirve	ellos sirven
ninguno *(adj.)*	no, nobody
ante *(prep.)*	before, in the presence of
perder	to lose
yo pierdo	nosotros perdemos
tú pierdes	vosotros perdéis
él pierde	ellos pierden

cultura *(f.n.)*	culture
forma *(f.n.)*	form
arte *(m.n.) (s.)*	art
artes *(f.n.) (pl.)*	
ésta *(pron.)*	this (one)
solo *(adj.)*	single, sole
quién *(pron.)*	who?
claro *(adj.)*	clear, bright, light
más *(adj.)*	more
tratar	to treat, handle
estudio *(m.n.)*	study
hacia *(prep.)*	towards
seis *(num.)*	six
medio *(adj.)*	half, average
razón *(f.n.)*	reason, ratio
lugar *(m.n.)*	place
buscar	to seek
camino *(m.n.)*	way, road
realidad *(f.n.)*	reality
mañana *(f.n.)*	morning, tomorrow
fuerza *(f.n.)*	strenght, force, power

Unit 12

alto *(adj.)*	high, tall
formar	to form
durante *(adv.)*	during
traer	to bring, carry
yo traigo	nosotros traemos
tú traes	vosotros traéis
él trae	ellos traen
cuando *(conj.)*	when
mejor *(adj.)*	better
allí *(adv.)*	there
guerra *(f.n.)*	war
leer	to read
yo leo	nosotros leemos
tú lees	vosotros leéis
él lee	ellos leen
ocho *(num.)*	eight
hallar	to find
gobierno *(m.n.)*	government
gracia *(f.n.)*	grace, kindness, wit (pl. thanks)
carácter *(m.n.)*	character
época *(f.n.)*	period
dentro *(adv.)*	inside
contra *(prep.)*	against
lado *(m.n.)*	side
bajo *(adv.)*	down, below
tarde *(f.n.)*	afternoon

Unit 13

persona *(f.n.)*	person
empezar	to begin
yo empiezo	nosotros empezamos
tú empicccs	vosotros empezáis
él empiece	ellos empiezan
presentar	to present
vario *(adj.)*	varied, variable
malo *(adj.)*	bad, wretched, unpleasant
gente *(f.n.)*	people
problema *(m.n.)*	problem
hija *(f.n.)*	daughter
antiguo *(adj.)*	ancient, old
nueve *(num.)*	nine
mes *(m.n.)*	month
alma *(f.n.)*	soul, spirit
dicho *(adj.)*	said, above-mentioned
color *(m.n.)*	colour
todavía *(adv.)*	still, yet
hecho *(m.n.)*	deed, act, fact
número *(m.n.)*	number
cuerpo *(m.n.)*	body
según *(prep.)*	according to
morir	to die
yo muero	nosotros morimos
tú mueres	vosotros morís
él muere	ellos mueren

Unit 14

vaso *(m.n.)*	glass
general *(adj.)*	general
pedir	to ask for
yo pido	nosotros pedimos
tú pides	vosotros pedís
él pide	ellos piden
gustar	to please ('me gusta', 'it pleases me', 'I like')
poco *(adv.)*	little, not much
además *(adv.)*	moreover
faltar	to lack
niño *(m.n.)*	boy, child
novela *(f.n.)*	novel
recibir	to receive
corazón *(m.n.)*	heart
andar	to go
tipo *(m.n.)*	type
segundo *(adj.)*	second
caer	to fall
yo caigo	nosotros caemos
tú caes	vosotros caéis
él cae	ellos caen
viejo *(adj.)*	old
comprender	to understand
sentido *(m.n.)*	meaning

Unit 15

algo *(pron.)*	anything, something
igual *(adj.)*	equal
humano *(adj.)*	human
campo *(m.n.)*	field, country(side)
pequeño *(adj.)*	small
elemento *(m.n.)*	element
exister	to exist
clase *(f.n.)*	class(room)
puerta *(f.n.)*	door(way), gate(way)
ocurrir	yo occur
cuyo *(pron.)*	whose, of which
relación *(f.n.)*	relation(ship)
necesitar	to need
poeta *(m.n., f.n.)* (also *f.n.* poetisa)	poet
valor *(m.n.)*	value, courage
político *(adj.)*	political
producir	to produce
posible *(adj.)*	possible
tanto *(adv.)*	as much, so much
recordar	to remember, remind

Unit 16

línea *(f.n.)*	line
objeto *(m.n.)*	object
ahí *(adv.)*	there
cabeza *(f.n.)*	head
aire *(m.n.)*	air
pronto *(adv.)*	quickly, early
ejemplo *(m.n.)*	example
doña *(f.n.)*	Mrs
doctor *(m.n.)*	doctor
mar *(m.n.)*	sea
blanco *(adj.)*	white
largo *(adj.)*	long
pobre *(adj.)*	poor
península *(f.n.)*	peninsula
comenzar	to begin
yo comienzo	nosotros comenzamos
tú comienzas	vosotros comenzáis
él comienza	ellos comienzan
siguiente *(adj.)*	following
callar	to be quiet
embargo *(m.n.)*	embargo, seizure ('sin embargo', 'however')
cuenta *(f.n.)*	account
explicar	to explain

Unit 17

cuya *(pron.)*	whose, of which
región *(f.n.)*	region
referir	to refer
yo refiero	nosotros referimos
tú refieres	vosotros referís
él refiere	ellos refieren
preguntar	to ask
verdadero *(adj.)*	true, truthful, real
maestro *(m.n.)*	master, teacher
interés *(m.n.)*	interest
efecto *(m.n.)*	effect
fondo *(m.n.)*	back(ground), bottom, fund
español *(m.n.)*	Spaniard (male)
natural *(adj.)*	natural
pie *(m.n.)*	feet
ofrecer	to offer
yo ofrezco	nosotros ofrecemos
tú ofreces	vosotros ofrecéis
él ofrece	ellos ofrecen
medio *(m.n.)*	middle, medium
noticia *(f.n.)*	notice, *(pl.)* news
república *(f.n.)*	republic
manera *(f.n.)*	way, manner
considerar	to consider
abrir	to open
único *(adj.)*	only, unique

Unit 18

correr	to run
voz *(f.n.)*	voice
pensamiento *(m.n.)*	thought
acción *(f.n.)*	action
por qué *(adv.)*	why
estudiar	to study
duda *(f.n.)*	doubt
frente *(m.n.)*	front, face
social *(adj.)*	social
real *(adj.)*	royal, real
público *(adj.)*	public
imagen *(f.n.)*	image, picture
crear	to create
conseguir	to get, bring about
yo consigo	nosotros conseguimos
tú consigues	vosotros conseguís
él consigue	ellos consiguen
distinto *(adj.)*	distinct, different
soler (+ infinitive)	to be in the habit of
yo suelo	nosotros solemos
tú sueles	vosotros soléis
él suele	ellos suelen
francés *(adj.)*	French
caballero *(m.n.)*	gentleman, rider
sol *(m.n.)*	sun
siete *(num.)*	seven

Unit 19

rey *(m.n.)*	king
familia *(f.n.)*	family
entender	to understand
yo entiendo	nosotros entendemos
tú entiendes	vosotros entendéis
él entiende	ellos entienden
olvidar	to forget
paso *(m.n.)*	step, passage, walk
dinero *(m.n.)*	money
publicar	to publish
algo *(adv.)*	rather, a bit
lleno *(adj.)*	full
ocupar	to occupy, employ
preciso *(adj.)*	necessary, exact
muerte *(f.n.)*	death
nacional *(adj.)*	national
cambio *(m.n.)*	exchange, change
resultar	to result
principio *(m.n.)*	beginning, principle
tampoco *(adv.)*	neither
centro *(m.n.)*	centre
marchar	to go, function, march
río *(m.n.)*	river

Unit 20

causa *(f.n.)*	cause
cara *(f.n.)*	face, appearance
cielo *(m.n.)*	sky, heaven
levantar	to raise (up)
condición *(f.n.)*	condition
brazo *(m.n.)*	arm
quizá(s) *(adv.)*	perhaps
dormir	to sleep
duermo	dormimos
duermes	dormís
duerme	duermen
descripción *(f.n.)*	description
anterior *(adj.)*	former, previous, front
nacer	to be born
nazco	nacemos
naces	nacéis
nace	nacen
mientras *(adv.)*	(mean)while
sacar	to get out, extract
marido *(m.n.)*	husband
echar	to throw, cast
permitir	to permit
literario *(adj.)*	literary
ministro *(m.n.)*	minister
trabajar	to work
suelo *(m.n.)*	ground, floor

detener	to delay, hold up
detengo	detenemos
detienes	detenéis
detiene	detienen
viaje *(m.n.)*	journey, trip
treinta *(num.)*	thirty
lejos *(adv.)*	far away
joven (m.n., f.n.)	young man, young woman
partido *(m.n.)*	party, match
casar	to marry
poco (un) *(m.n.)*	(a) little
representar	to represent, perform
universidad *(f.n.)*	university
derecho *(m.n.)*	law, right, duty, straight
carta *(f.n.)*	card, letter
origen *(m.n.)*	origin
suponer	to suppose
supongo	suponemos
supones	suponéis
supone	suponen
edad *(f.n.)*	age
papel *(m.n.)*	paper, role
negro *(adj.)*	black
falta *(f.n.)*	lack, failure, fault
médico *(m.n.)*	doctor
ganar	to earn, gain, win

Unit 22

hermano *(m.n.)*	brother
movimiento *(m.n.)*	movement
escuela *(f.n.)*	school
científico *(adj.)*	scientific
moderno *(adj.)*	modern
otra *(pron.)*	(an)other *(f.)*
término *(m.n.)*	end, boundary, term
puro *(adj.)*	pure
figura *(f.n.)*	figure
método *(m.n.)*	method
ayer *(adv.)*	yesterday
actual *(adj.)*	present, current
general *(m.n.)*	general
sentimiento *(m.n.)*	feeling, emotion
continuar	to continue
motivo *(m.n.)*	reason, motive
gusto *(m.n.)*	taste, pleasure
comer	to eat
repetir	to repeat
repito	repetimos
repites	repetís
repite	repiten
zona *(f.n.)*	zone

¡ay! *(int.)*	oh!
mismo *(pron.)*	self (' yo mismo ', 'I myself')
poder *(m.n.)*	power
ésa *(pron.)*	that (one), the former (f.)
función *(f.n.)*	function, performance
ocasión *(f.n.)*	occasion
convenir	to agree, be good for
convengo	convenimos
convienes	convenís
conviene	convienen
sentar	to sit, settle
siento	sentamos
sientas	sentáis
sienta	sientan
terminar	to complete, stop
próximo *(adj.)*	near, next
sociedad *(f.n.)*	society
cuestión *(f.n.)*	matter, quarrel
valer	to be worth(y), equal, protect
allá *(adv.)*	there
flor *(f.n.)*	flower
oro *(m.n.)*	gold
diez *(num.)*	ten
provincia *(f.n.)*	province
tocar	to play, touch, concern
demostrar	to demonstrate, to show
demuestro	demostramos
demuestras	demostráis
demuestra	demuestran

lector *(m.n.)*	reader
televisión *(f.n.)*	television
mandar	to order, send, be in command
rico *(adj.)*	rich
hermana *(f.n.)*	sister
acto *(m.n.)*	act(ion), deed
señorita *(f.n.)*	miss, young lady
servicio *(m.n.)*	service
bastar	to suffice
difícil *(adj.)*	difficult
histórico *(adj.)*	historic(al)
desear	to desire
profundo *(adj.)*	deep
conocido *(adj.)*	(well-)known
fuera *(adv.)*	out(side), away
escritor *(m.n.)*	writer
llorar	to weep
política *(f.n.)*	politics
reconocer	to recognise
reconozco	reconocemos
reconoces	reconocéis
reconoce	reconocen
opinión *(f.n.)*	opinion

libre *(adj.)*	free
mostrar	to show
muestro	mostramos
muestras	mostráis
muestra	muestran
artículo *(m.n.)*	article
importancia *(f.n.)*	importance
revolución *(f.n.)*	revolution
matar	to kill
¡ah! *(int.)*	ah!
suceder	to happen, succeed
cambiar	to (ex)change
feliz *(adj.)*	happy
sufrir	to suffer
constituir	to constitute
constituyo	constituimos
constituyes	constituís
constituye	constituyen
llamado *(adj.)*	called
iglesia *(f.n.)*	church
poseer	to possess
hotel *(m.n.)*	hotel
triste *(adj.)*	sad
conocimiento *(m.n.)*	knowledge, acquaintance
celebrar	to celebrate
geografía *(f.n.)*	geography

pesar	to weigh
valle *(m.n.)*	valley
autoridad *(f.n.)*	authority
añadir	to add
conservar	to preserve, keep
posición *(f.n.)*	position
defender	to defend
defiendo	defendemos
defiendes	defendéis
defiende	defienden
niña *(f.n.)*	girl, child (f.)
concepto *(m.n.)*	concept(ion)
demás *(pron.)*	rest, others
importante *(adj.)*	important
principal *(adj.)*	principal
fijar	to fix
propósito *(m.n.)*	purpose, intention
piedra *(f.n.)*	stone
situación *(f.n.)*	situation
una *(pron.)*	somebody (f.)
necesario *(adj.)*	necessary
serie *(f.n.)*	series
mal *(adv.)*	badly

observar	to observe
cuarto *(m.n.)*	room, quarter
sistema *(m.n.)*	system
hecho *(adj.)*	complete, done
aspecto *(m.n.)*	appearance, aspect
sombra *(f.n.)*	shade, shadow
adquirir	to acquire
adquiero	adquirimos
adquieres	adquirís
adquiere	adquieren
especie *(f.n.)*	species
población *(f.n.)*	population, hamlet
boca *(f.n.)*	mouth
tercero *(adj.)*	third
personaje *(m.n.)*	celebrity, character
cualquier *(pron.)*	anybody, whichever
subir	to raise, go up, climb
ambos *(adj.)*	both
recoger	to gather, pick up
recojo	recogemos
recoges	recogéis
recoge	recogen
mesa *(f.n.)*	table
paz *(f.n.)*	peace
pasado *(adj.)*	past
minuto *(m.n.)*	minute

Unit 28

dirigir	to direct, manage, drive
dirijo	dirigimos
diriges	dirigís
dirige	dirigen
reír	to laugh
río	reímos
ríes	reís
ríe	ríen
completo *(adj.)*	complete, inclusive, full
proponer	to propose
propongo	proponemos
propones	proponéis
propone	proponen
importar	to be important, amount to, import
teatro *(m.n.)*	theatre
asunto *(m.n.)*	matter, subject
capítulo *(m.n.)*	chapter
existencia *(f.n.)*	existence
etcétera *(adv.)*	and so on
figurar	to figure, represent
meter	to put, place
aspecto *(m.n.)*	appearance, aspect
destino *(m.n.)*	destiny, destination
interesar	to interest
necesidad *(f.n.)*	need
diverso *(adj.)*	different, several
advertir	to notice, point out
advierto	advertimos
adviertes	advertís
advierte	advierten
plaza *(f.n.)*	square, place, job
literatura *(f.n.)*	literature

Unit 29

indicar	to indicate
periódico *(m.n.)*	journal
investigación *(f.n.)*	investigation
afirmar	to state, make steady
extraordinario *(adj.)*	extraordinary
pagar	to pay
lograr	to obtain, achieve
especial *(adj.)*	(e)special
capital *(m.n.)*	capital
nación *(f.n.)*	nation
veinte *(num.)*	twenty
popular *(adj.)*	popular
emplear	to employ, use
quitar	to take off, take away
artista (m.n., f.n.)	artist
pretender	to try to, claim
hermoso *(adj.)*	beautiful, handsome
cerca *(adv.)*	nearby
frase *(f.n.)*	sentence, quotation
escuchar	to listen (to)

Unit 30

árbol *(m.n.)*	tree
libertad *(f.n.)*	freedom
corresponder	to correspond, belong
acercar	to bring near
ventana *(f.n.)*	window
deseo *(m.n.)*	wish, desire
página *(f.n.)*	page
azul *(adj.)*	blue
acudir	to come (along), (up)
dirección *(f.n.)*	address, direction
estación *(f.n.)*	station, season
honor *(m.n.)*	honour
raro *(adj.)*	rare
exponer	to expose, expound, exhibit
expongo	exponemos
expones	exponéis
expone	exponen
acaso *(adv.)*	perhaps
precisamente	precisely
consistir	to consist
memoria *(f.n.)*	memory, report
descubrir	to discover
describir	to describe

acompañar	to accompany
cantar	to singer
comprar	to buy
común *(adj.)*	common
ser *(m.n.)*	being
bajar	to lower, bring down
religioso *(adj.)*	religious
reino *(m.n.)*	kingdom
norte *(m.n.)*	north
perdonar	to excuse, pardon
dolor *(m.n.)*	sorrow, pain
intelectual *(m.n.)*	intellectual
obrero *(m.n.)*	worker, labourer
naturaleza *(f.n.)*	nature
bello *(adj.)*	beautiful
visitar	to visit
cumplir	to carry out, fulfil
secreto *(m.n.)*	secret
guardar	to guard, keep
sangre *(m.n.)*	blood

Unit 32

masa *(f.n.)*	mass
apenas *(adv.)*	hardly
silencio *(m.n.)*	silence
millón *(m.n.)*	million
voluntad *(f.n.)*	will
esfuerzo *(m.n.)*	effort
favor *(m.n.)*	favour, service ('por favor', 'please')
intentar	to attempt, intend
alcanzar	to catch (up) (with), manage
círculo *(m.n.)*	circle
aparato *(m.n.)*	apparatus
superior *(adj.)*	upper, higher, superior
decidir	to decide
atención *(f.n.)*	attention
según *(adv.)*	it depends
conciencia *(f.n.)*	conscience
extraño *(adj.)*	strange
muchacha *(f.n.)*	girl
público *(m.n.)*	public
mantener	to maintain
mantengo	mantenemos
mantienes	mantenéis
mantiene	mantienen

discurso *(m.n.)*	speech, passage
toro *(m.n.)*	bull
juventud *(f.n.)*	youth
pasión *(f.n.)*	passion
técnica *(f.n.)*	technique, technology
disponer	to dispose, prepare
dispongo	disponemos
dispones	disponéis
dispone	disponen
instrumento *(m.n.)*	instrument
emoción *(f.n.)*	emotion
costa *(f.n.)*	coast, cost
fiesta *(f.n.)*	party, feast, festival
costumbre *(f.n.)*	custom, habit
merecer	to deserve
merezco	merecemos
mereces	merecéis
merece	merecen
mirada *(f.n.)*	glance, look
prueba *(f.n.)*	proof, test
nervioso *(adj.)*	nervous
suerte *(f.n.)*	luck
significar	to mean
espectáculo *(m.n.)*	spectacle, show
corriente *(f.n.)*	current
vivo *(adj.)*	living, lively

Unit 34

aceptar	to accept
fuego *(m.n.)*	fire
asegurar	to assure
interesante *(adj.)*	interesting
fuerte *(adj.)*	strong
observación *(f.n.)*	observation
coche *(m.n.)*	car, coach
simple *(adj.)*	simple
alguno *(pron.)*	some(one)
grave *(adj.)*	heavy, serious
género *(m.n.)*	class, genre, gender
notar	to note
seguro *(adj.)*	sure
justicia *(f.n.)*	justice
texto *(m.n.)*	text
aquél *(pron.)*	that (one)
objetivo *(m.n.)*	objective
grado *(m.n.)*	degree, step
recuerdo *(m.n.)*	memory, souvenir
obtener	to obtain
obtengo	obtenemos
obtienes	obtenéis
obtiene	obtienen

numeroso *(adj.)*	numerous
palacio *(m.n.)*	palace
contestar	to answer
tema *(m.n.)*	thcme
alegría *(f.n.)*	happiness
asistir	to be present, attend
régimen *(m.n.)*	diet, régime
encima *(adv.)*	on top, above
puesto *(adj.)*	(clothes) wearing, (table) laid
miedo *(m.n.)*	fear
gloria *(f.n.)*	glory
letra *(f.n.)*	letter
mover	to move
muevo	movemos
mueves	movéis
mueve	mueven
militar *(adj.)*	military
vender	to sell
árabe *(adj.)*	Arab, Arabic
título *(m.n.)*	title
colocar	to place, put
responder	to reply
consejo *(m.n.)*	advice

Unit 36

bueno *(adj.)*	good
instante *(m.n.)*	instant
inglés *(adj.)*	English
menor *(adj.)*	minor, smaller, smallest, less, least
civil *(adj.)*	civil
nota *(f.n.)*	note, mark
jardín *(m.n.)*	garden
peseta *(f.n.)*	peseta
consecuencia *(f.n.)*	consequence
semana *(f.n.)*	week
sueño *(m.n.)*	sleep, dream
enseñar	to teach, train, show
ambiente *(m.n.)*	environment, atmosphere
labor *(f.n.)*	work, job
teoría *(f.n.)*	theory
cerrar	to close
cierro	cerramos
cierras	cerráis
cierra	cierran
asimismo *(adv.)*	in the same way
cuidado *(m.n.)*	care
respecto *(m.n.)*	respect
compañero *(m.n.)*	companion, mate

fácil *(adj.)*	easy
héroe *(m.n.)*	hero
ligero *(m.n.)*	light
balcón *(m.n.)*	balcony
lucha *(f.n.)*	struggle
experiencia *(f.n.)*	experience, experiment
señalar	to mark, point (out), (to)
influencia *(f.n.)*	influence
convertir	to convert
convierto	convertimos
conviertes	convertís
convierte	convierten
ejército *(m.n.)*	army
huir	to flee
huyo	huimos
huyes	huís
huye	huyen
manifestación *(f.n.)*	sign, declaration, rally
través *(m.n.)*	bend, bias, reverse
preparar	to prepare
actividad *(f.n.)*	activity
rato *(m.n.)*	while, period
contemplar	to contemplate
quince *(num.)*	fifteen
tarde *(adv.)*	late
enorme *(adj.)*	enormous

Unit 38

duro *(adj.)*	hard
enemigo *(m.n.)*	enemy
organización *(f.n.)*	organization
partir	set off, start, split (open)
jefe (m.n., f.n.)	chief, head
resultado *(m.n.)*	result
perfecto *(adj.)*	perfect
reducir	to reduce
reduzco	reducimos
reduces	reducís
reduce	reducen
dama *(f.n.)*	lady
bajo *(adj.)*	low, short
negar	to deny, refuse
niego	negamos
niegas	negáis
niega	niegan
juzgar	to judge
curva *(f.n.)*	curve
imponer	to impose
impongo	imponemos
impones	imponéis
impone	imponen
aprendar	to learn
demás *(adj.)*	other, rest (of them)
uso *(m.n.)*	use
plano *(m.n.)*	plan, plane
cuento *(m.n.)*	story
ija! (interj.)	ha!

jugar	to play
juego	jugamos
juegas	jugáis
juega	juegan
demasiado *(adj.)*	too
mejor *(adv.)*	better
exacto *(adj.)*	correct, exact
retrato *(m.n.)*	portrait
error *(m.n.)*	error
impresión *(f.n.)*	impression
actitud *(f.n.)*	attitude
matrimonio *(m.n.)*	marriage, married couple
cuadro *(m.n.)*	square, picture
instinto *(m.n.)*	instinct
bastante *(adj.)*	sufficient
sostener	to sustain
sostengo	sostenemos
sostienes	sostenéis
sostiene	sostienen
acuerdo *(m.n.)*	agreement, sense(s)
espacio *(m.n.)*	space
patria *(f.n.)*	native land
¡oh! (interj.)	oh!
solución *(f.n.)*	solution
fecha *(f.n.)*	date
ochenta *(num.)*	eighty

Unit 40

amar	to love
sitio *(m.n.)*	place
llenar	to fill
fe *(f.n.)*	faith
vital *(adj.)*	living, vital
presente *(adj.)*	present
disposición *(f.n.)*	disposition
fortuna *(f.n.)*	fortune
expresión *(f.n.)*	expression
pleno *(adj.)*	full
habitación *(f.n.)*	room, dwelling
juicio *(m.n.)*	judgment, reason, opinion
medida *(f.n.)*	size, measure(ment)
establecer	to establish
establezco	establecemos
estableces	establecéis
establece	establecen
salvar	to save, reach
particular *(adj.)*	private, particular
jamás *(adv.)*	never
convencer	to convince
convenzo	convencemos
convences	convencéis
convence	convencen
guardia *(f.n.) (m.n.)*	guard, police(woman), policeman
procurar	to try, get, manage (to)

clásico *(adj.)*	classical
desaparecer	to disappear
desaparezco	desaparecemos
desapareces	desaparecéis
desaparece	desaparecen
ilusión *(f.n.)*	illusion
peligro *(m.n.)*	danger
carne *(f.n.)*	meat, flesh
verso *(m.n.)*	verse, line (of poetry)
visión *(f.n.)*	vision
convento *(m.n.)*	monastery; (de monjas, nunnery)
dulce *(adj.)*	sweet, gentle
exigir	to demand, need
exijo	exigimos
exiges	exigís
exige	exigen
base *(f.n.)*	base, basis
determinado *(adj.)*	fixed, certain
arma *(f.n.)*	arm, weapon
raza *(f.n.)*	race
compañía *(f.n.)*	company
tía *(f.n.)*	aunt
dedicar	to dedicate
suma *(f.n.)*	sum(mary)
detalle *(m.n.)*	detail, gesture, bill
octavo *(adj.)*	eighth

Unit 42

central *(adj.)*	central
café *(m.n.)*	coffee, café
diferencia *(f.n.)*	difference
tradición *(f.n.)*	tradition
acerca *(adv.)*	approximately
republicano *(adj.)*	republican
construcción *(f.n.)*	construction
prestar	to lend
entero *(adj.)*	whole, entire
citar	to cite, make an appointment
ideal *(m.n.)*	ideal
academia *(f.n.)*	academy
límite *(m.n.)*	limit, extreme
planta *(f.n.)*	plan(t), storey
pobre *(adj.)*	poor
absoluto *(adj.)*	absolute
eterno *(adj.)*	eternal
barco *(m.n.)*	boat, ship
mayoría *(f.n.)*	majority
construir	to construct
construyo	construimos
construyes	construís
construye	construyen

breve *(adj.)*	short, brief
coger	to take hold of, pick (up), catch (up) (with)
cojo	cogemos
coges	cogéis
coge	cogen
creación *(f.n.)*	creation
declarar	to declare
verde *(adj.)*	green
caber	to go (in), fit, happen
quepo	cobemos
cabes	cabéis
cabe	caben
alegre *(adj.)*	happy, merry
delante *(adv.)*	in front, ahead
jurar	to swear
geográfico *(adj.)*	geographic(al)
despertar	to wake (up), awaken
despierto	despertamos
despiertas	despertáis
despierta	despiertan
extranjero *(adj.)*	foreign
magnífico *(adj.)*	magnificent
plan *(m.n.)*	plan, basis
físico *(adj.)*	physical
juego *(m.n.)*	game, set, play
práctico *(adj.)*	practical
desarrollo *(m.n.)*	development
junta *(f.n.)*	meeting, commitee, junta
reunir	to gather, assemble, get together

Unit 44

distancia *(f.n.)*	distance
artístico *(adj.)*	artistic
hoja *(f.n.)*	leaf, sheet
famoso *(adj.)*	famous
junto *(adv.)*	together
dificultad *(f.n.)*	difficulty
pared *(f.n.)*	wall
labio *(m.n.)*	lip
escena *(f.n.)*	scene, stage
conversación *(f.n.)*	conversation
santa *(f.n.)*	(female) saint
corte *(f.n.)*	court (Cortes, Parliament)
gozar	to enjoy
belleza *(f.n.)*	beauty
proceder	to proceed
presidente (m.n., f.n.)	president
capitán *(m.n.)*	captain
ancho *(adj.)*	broad, wide
obligar	to oblige
dato *(m.n.)*	fact

solamente *(adv.)*	only
leyenda *(f.n.)*	legend
lengua *(f.n.)*	tongue, language
imaginar	to imagine
matemática *(f.n.)*	mathematics
cortar	to cut
muchacho *(m.n.)*	boy, lad
propiedad *(f.n.)*	property, accuracy
gesto *(m.n.)*	face, gesture
montaña *(f.n.)*	mountain
hogar *(m.n.)*	fireplace, home
vuestro *(adj.)*	your
avanzar	to advance, promote
entregar	to deliver, hand (over), (in)
materia *(f.n.)*	material, matter
extender	to extend
extiendo	extendemos
extiendes	extendéis
extiende	extienden
nuevo *(m.n.)*	(the) new
plata *(f.n.)*	money, silver
adelante *(adv.)*	forward, onward, ahead
aumentar	to increase

Unit 46

enfermo *(adj.)*	ill
puerto *(m.n.)*	port
espiritual *(adj.)*	spiritual
lectura *(f.n.)*	reading
contener	to contain
contengo	contenemos
contienes	contenéis
contiene	contienen
lente (m.n., f.n.)	lens
cualquiera *(pron.)*	whatever, whoever
moral *(adj.)*	moral
cabo *(m.n.)*	end, cape
pertenecer	to belong
pertenezco	pertenecemos
perteneces	pertenecéis
pertenece	pertenecen
tren *(m.n.)*	train
defensa *(f.n.)*	defence
profesor *(m.n.)*	teacher, professor (m.)
profesora *(f.n.)*	teacher, professor (f.)
enfermedad *(f.n.)*	illness
precioso *(f.n.)*	precious
rostro *(m.n.)*	face
comunicar	to communicate
dado *(adj.)*	given
civilización *(f.n.)*	civilization
fino *(adj.)*	fine refined

mucho *(pron.)*	a lot
surgir	to spring (up), arise
surjo	surgimos
surges	surgís
surge	surgen
abandonar	to abandon
estructura *(f.n.)*	structure
verano *(m.n.)*	summer
maravilloso *(adj.)*	wonderful
evitar	to avoid
tranquilo *(adj.)*	calm
curso *(m.n.)*	course
precio *(m.n.)*	price
culpa *(f.n.)*	blame, guilt, sin
sabio *(m.n.)*	scholar, wise man
europeo *(adj.)*	European
loco *(adj.)*	mad
naturalmente *(adv.)*	naturally
unido *(adj.)*	united
estilo *(m.n.)*	style
pena *(f.n.)*	grief, trouble, punishment
ángel *(m.n.)*	angel, charm
príncipe *(m.n.)*	prince

Unit 48

espejo *(m.n.)*	mirror
prensa *(f.n.)*	press
edificio *(m.n.)*	building
oficial *(adj.)*	official
revista *(f.n.)*	review
frecuencia *(f.n.)*	frequency
temer	to fear
grito *(m.n.)*	shout, cry
divino *(adj.)*	divine
capaz *(adj.)*	capable, capacious
romper	to break
curiosidad *(f.n.)*	curiosity
eje *(m.n.)*	axis, axle
íntimo *(adj.)*	intimate
sonar	to play, sound
sueno	sonamos
suuenas	sonáis
suena	suenan
negocio *(m.n.)*	affair, business, deal
tirar	to throw (away), shoot, pull
distinguir	to distinguish
distingo	distinguimos
distingues	distinguís
distingue	distinguen
substancia *(f.n.)*	substance
conferencia *(f.n.)*	conference

chico *(m.n.)*	boy, lad
diferente *(adj.)*	different
pecho *(m.n.)*	chest, breast
luminoso *(adj.)*	bright, shining
respeto *(m.n.)*	respect
amplio *(adj.)*	ample, spacious
superficie *(f.n.)*	surface
engañar	to deceive, mislead
modelo *(m.n.)*	model
hambre *(f.n.)*	hunger
inteligencia *(f.n.)*	intelligence
muerto *(adj.)*	dead
personal *(adj.)*	personal
ayudar	to help
corto *(adj.)*	short
pregunta *(f.n.)*	question
terrible *(adj.)*	terrible
crítica *(f.n.)*	criticism
ignorar	not to know
directo *(adj.)*	direct

Unit 50

preferir	to prefer
prefiero	preferimos
prefieres	preferís
prefiere	prefieren
doce *(m.n.)*	twelve
abierto *(adj.)*	open
beber	to drink
fantasía *(f.n.)*	fantasy
inmenso *(adj.)*	immense
seguida *(f.n.)*	proper way (en seguida, right away)
tabla *(f.n.)*	board, shelf, table
visita *(f.n.)*	visit
atreverse	to dare
impedir	to hinder
impido	impedimos
impides	impedís
impide	impiden
matemático *(adj.)*	mathematical
novio *(f.n.)*	fiancé, sweetheart, bridegroom
suceso *(m.n.)*	incident, event
amo *(m.n.)*	master, owner
suave *(adj.)*	gentle, mild
piel *(f.n.)*	skin
laboratorio *(m.n.)*	laboratory
detrás *(adv.)*	behind
especialmente *(adv.)*	especially

rojo *(adj.)*	red
alemán *(adj.)*	German
deber *(m.n.)*	duty, debt
esencial *(adj.)*	essential
perfectamente *(adv.)*	perfectly
caballo *(m.n.)*	horse
enviar	to send
envío	enviamos
envías	enviáis
envía	envían
sensación *(f.n.)*	sensation
arrancar	to spring (up, out), tear (away, off), snatch
pan *(m.n.)*	bread, loaf
puesto *(m.n.)*	position, post
bonito *(adj.)*	pretty
carrera *(f.n.)*	race, run, rush, route
continuación *(f.n.)*	continuation
mitad *(f.n.)*	half, middle
conforme *(adj.)*	agreed, alike, consistent
penetrar	to penetrate
lanzar	to throw (out, down, up)
demasiado *(adv.)*	too (much)
golpe *(m.n.)*	blow, coup

Unit 52

pelo *(m.n.)*	hair
individuo *(m.n.)*	individual
villa *(f.n.)*	villa, small town
hondo *(adj.)*	deep, low
dominar	to dominate
exposición *(f.n.)*	exhibition
vestido *(adj.)*	dressed
andaluz *(adj.)*	Andalusian
personalidad *(f.n.)*	personality
pieza *(f.n.)*	piece, room, play
pasado *(m.n.)*	past
unidad *(f.n.)*	unit(y)
remedio *(m.n.)*	remedy
inglés *(m.n.)*	Englishman
seco *(adj.)*	dry, brusque
conde *(m.n.)*	count
dudar	to doubt
terreno *(m.n.)*	(piece of) land, ground
ánimos *(m.n.)*	mind, spirit, courage
vuelta *(f.n.)*	turn, bend

representación *(f.n.)*	representation, performance
novelista (m.n., f.n.)	novelist
cristal *(m.n.)*	glass, crystal
serio *(adj.)*	serious
columna *(f.n.)*	column
filosofía *(f.n.)*	philosophy
debajo *(adv.)*	under(neath)
pluma *(f.n.)*	pen, feather
limitar	to limit
acordar(se)	to agree, decide, recall
acuerdo	acordamos
acuerdas	acordáis
acuerda	acuerdan
resto *(m.n.)*	rest, (restos, remains)
completamente *(adv.)*	completely
domingo *(m.n.)*	Sunday
fórmula *(f.n.)*	formula
imposible *(adj.)*	impossible
escapar	to escape
seguramente *(adv.)*	surely
porvenir *(m.n.)*	future
medicina *(f.n.)*	medicine
mío *(pron.)*	mine

Unit 54

traje *(m.n.)*	dress, suit
producto *(m.n.)*	product
curioso *(adj.)*	curious
económico *(adj.)*	economic(al)
noble *(adj.)*	noble
ibérico *(adj.)*	Iberian
joven *(adj.)*	young
mañana *(adv.)*	tomorrow
junto *(adj.)*	together, next to
fuente *(f.n.)*	spring, fount(ain)
marquesa *(f.n.)*	marchioness
presencia *(f.n.)*	presence
viajero *(m.n.)*	traveller
raíz *(f.n.)*	root
socialista (m.n., f.n.)	socialist
criatura *(f.n.)*	creature
extremo *(m.n.)*	extreme
universal *(adj.)*	universal
cultural *(adj.)*	cultural
éxito *(m.n.)*	success, result

soldado *(m.n.)*	soldier
examinar	to examine
francés *(m.n.)*	Frenchman
cuanto *(pron.)*	as much as
generación *(f.n.)*	generation
poesía *(f.n.)*	poetry, poem
unir	to unite
anoche *(adv.)*	last night
metal *(m.n.)*	metal
religión *(f.n.)*	religion
sorprender	to surprise
criterio *(m.n.)*	criterion
interpretación *(f.n.)*	interpretation
definición *(f.n.)*	definition
separar	to separate
viejo *(adj.)*	old
extensión *(f.n.)*	extention
industria *(f.n.)*	industry
cantidad *(f.n.)*	quantity
mamá *(f.n.)*	mummy, mom

parar	to stop, parry
comercio *(m.n.)*	commerce
riqueza *(f.n.)*	wealth
cama *(f.n.)*	bed
gris *(adj.)*	grey
tender	to spread (out), stretch (out), tend
tiendo	tendemos
tiendes	tendéis
tiende	tienden
humanidad *(f.n.)*	humanity
comedia *(f.n.)*	comedy
lejano *(adj.)*	distant
tendencia *(f.n.)*	tendency
viento *(m.n.)*	wind
resolver	to (re)solve
resuelvo	resolvemos
resuelves	resolvéis
resuelve	resuelven
usar	to use
categoría *(f.n.)*	category
música *(f.n.)*	music
desarrollar	to develop, unfold
alguien *(pron.)*	someone, anybody
sencillo *(adj.)*	simple
triunfo *(m.n.)*	triumph
apuntar	to point (at), (to), (out), note (down), show

expresar	to express
material *(m.n.)*	material(s), equipment
señorito *(m.n.)*	young gentleman
brillante *(adj.)*	brilliant
fenómeno *(m.n.)*	phenomenon
habitante (m.n., f.n.)	inhabitant
¿adonde? *(adv.)*	where?
cerrado *(adj.)*	closed, thick, overcast
manifestar	to show, reveal
manifiesto	manifestamos
manifiestas	manifestáis
manifiesta	manifiestan
semejante *(adj.)*	similar
genio *(m.n.)*	genius, disposition
perro *(m.n.)*	dog
trasladar	to move, transfer, translate
aquélla *(pron.)*	that, former (f.)
conducir	to take, carry, drive, guide
conduzco	conducimos
conduces	conducís
conduce	conducen
cristiano *(adj.)*	Christian
facultad *(f.n.)*	faculty
cargo *(m.n.)*	charge, load, duty
mérito *(m.n.)*	merit
acostar	to lay down, lie down
acuesto	acostamos
acuestas	acostáis
acuesta	acuestan

felicidad *(f.n.)*	happiness
ángulo *(m.n.)*	angle, corner
muro *(m.n.)*	wall
actor *(m.n.)*	actor
comisión *(f.n.)*	commission
oficio *(m.n.)*	job, trade, office
aprovechar	to profit (by) (from), (be of) use
derecha *(f.n.)*	right (hand) (side)
doctrina *(f.n.)*	doctrine
territorio *(m.n.)*	territory
contrario *(m.n.)*	contrary
análogo *(adj.)*	analogous
fundamental *(adj.)*	fundamental
mentira *(f.n.)*	lie
asomar	to show
despedir	to say goodbye, see (off), (out), dismiss
despido	despedimos
despides	despedís
despide	despiden
ensayo *(m.n.)*	essay
ilustre *(adj.)*	illustrious
rosa *(f.n.)*	rose
mal *(m.n.)*	evil, misfortune, illness

tío *(m.n.)*	uncle
contemporáneo *(adj.)*	contemporary
fundar	to found
permanecer	to remain
permanezco	permanecemos
permaneces	permanecéis
permanece	permanecen
organizar	to organize
admirable *(adj.)*	admirable
causar	to cause
encerrar	to shut (up), (in), lock (up), (in), include
encierro	encerramos
encierras	encerráis
encierra	encierran
aplicación *(f.n.)*	application
bastante *(adv.)*	sufficiently
frontera *(f.n.)*	frontier
descubrimiento *(m.n.)*	discovery
boda *(f.n.)*	wedding, marriage
procedimiento *(m.n.)*	process, procedure
anunciar	to announce
romano *(adj.)*	Roman
ocultar	to hide
misterio *(m.n.)*	mystery
célula *(f.n.)*	cell
iniciar	to begin, initiate

Unit 60

circunstancia *(f.n.)*	circumstance
animal *(m.n.)*	animal
esperanza *(f.n.)*	hope
constante *(adj.)*	constant
frío *(adj.)*	cold
reciente *(adj.)*	recent
amistad *(f.n.)*	friendship
interior *(adj.)*	interior, inner
sala *(f.n.)*	room, hall
mas *(conj.)*	but
incluso *(adj.)*	enclosed, inclusive
museo *(m.n.)*	museum
aventura *(f.n.)*	adventure
griego *(adj.)*	Greek
justo *(adj.)*	just, right, exact
cubrir	to cover
baile *(m.n.)*	dance, ball, ballet
satisfacción *(f.n.)*	satisfaction
monte *(m.n.)*	mountain
lección *(f.n.)*	lesson, class

probar	to prove, try, test
pruebo	probamos
pruebas	probáis
prueba	prueban
romántico *(adj.)*	romantic
vera *(f.n.)*	edge, bank, border
sur *(m.n.)*	south
discutir	to discuss, argue (about), (against)
agradecer	to be grateful, thank
agradezco	agradecemos
agradeces	agradecéis
agradece	agradecen
papá *(m.n.)*	daddy, pop
suyo *(pron.)*	his, hers, its, yours, theirs
elegante *(adj.)*	elegant
isla *(f.n.)*	island
división *(f.n.)*	division
talento *(m.n.)*	talent
inquietud *(f.n.)*	worry, restlessness
comida *(f.n.)*	food, meal
intención *(f.n.)*	intention
setenta *(num.)*	seventy
torre *(f.n.)*	tower
bondad *(f.n.)*	goodness
conjunto *(m.n.)*	whole, ensemble
pronunciar	to pronounce

Unit 62

resistir	to resist
atravesar	to cross (over), lay across
atravieso	atravesamos
atraviesas	atravesáis
atraviesa	atraviesan
arriba *(adv.)*	above, overhead, up
paisaje *(m.n.)*	landscape
comienzo *(m.n.)*	beginning, inception
liberal *(adj.)*	liberal
dieciseis *(num.)*	sixteen
rayo *(m.n.)*	ray, lightning
marcha *(f.n.)*	march, walk, speed
apreciar	to appreciate
padecer	to suffer
padezco	padecemos
padeces	padecéis
padece	padecen
proceso *(m.n.)*	process(ing), trial
debido *(adj.)*	due, proper
broma *(f.n.)*	fun, joke
video *(m.n.)*	video (recorder)
tropa *(f.n.)*	troop, crowd
tropezar	to trip, run (into), (up against)
virtud *(f.n.)*	virtue
espalda *(f.n.)*	shoulder, back
madera *(f.n.)*	wood
gritar	to shout
falso *(adj.)*	false

ejemplar *(m.n.)*	example, copy, specimen
camarada (m.n., f.n.)	comrade, pal
contacto *(m.n.)*	contact
digno *(adj.)*	worthy
original *(adj.)*	original
ingenio *(m.n.)*	wit, ingenuity
borde *(m.n.)*	edge, border, side
confesar	to confess
confieso	confesamos
confiesas	confesáis
confiesa	confiesan
elevar	to raise, promote
cálculo *(m.n.)*	calculation
sonréir	to smile
sonrío	sonreímos
sonríes	sonréis
sonríe	sonríen
blanco *(m.n.)*	white(ness)
molestar	to annoy, disturb
altura *(f.n.)*	height, depth, latitude
crítico *(m.n.)*	critic
mencionar	to mention
tras *(prep.)*	behind, beyond, after
preocupación *(f.n.)*	preoccupation
duque *(m.n.)*	duke
regla *(f.n.)*	rule(r), regulation

Unit 64

pesar *(m.n.)*	regret, grief
comprobar	to check, prove
compruebo	comprobamos
compruebas	comprobáis
comprueba	comprueban
estrella *(f.n.)*	star
novedad *(f.n.)*	novelty
cruzar	to cross
rápido *(adj.)*	quick
volumen *(m.n.)*	volume
confianza *(f.n.)*	confidence, trust
biblioteca *(f.n.)*	library
componer	to compose
compongo	componemos
compones	componéis
compone	componen
filósofo *(m.n.)*	philosopher
vencer	to beat, win, conquer
venzo	vencemos
vences	vencéis
vence	vencen
remoto *(adj.)*	remote
profesión *(f.n.)*	profession
nada *(f.n.)*	nothingness, void
educar	to educate
dispuesto *(adj.)*	disposed
excelente *(adj.)*	excellent
italiano *(adj.)*	Italian
par *(m.n.)*	couple, pair

aquello *(pron.)*	that, former (m.)
satisfacer	to satisfy
satisfago	satisfacemos
satisfaces	satisfacćis
satisface	satisfacen
escrito *(adj.)*	written
definir	to define
once *(num.)*	eleven
tono *(m.n.)*	tone
cuidar	to care (for), (of), mind
historiador *(m.n.)*	historian
piso *(m.n.)*	floor, storey
arco *(m.n.)*	arc, arch(way)
costar	to cost
cuesto	costamos
cuestas	costáis
cuesta	cuestan
barba *(f.n.)*	beard
cincuenta *(num.)*	fifty
saludar	to greet
proyecto *(m.n.)*	project, plan
enseñanza *(f.n.)*	education, teaching
fruto *(m.n.)*	fruit
limpio *(adj.)*	clean
publicado *(adj.)*	published
entrada *(f.n.)*	entrance, entry

internacional *(adj.)*	international
querido *(adj.)*	dear, darling
energía *(f.n.)*	energy
conceder	to concede
fábrica *(f.n.)*	factory, manufacture
santo *(m.n.)*	saint
pintar	to paint
deducir	to deduce, deduct
deduzco	deducimos
deduces	deducís
deduce	deducen
cariño *(m.n.)*	affection, fondness
sección *(f.n.)*	section
atender	to attend (to), serve, care for
atiendo	atendemos
atiendes	atendéis
atiende	atienden
revolucionario *(adj.)*	revolutionary
cámara *(f.n.)*	chamber, room
oscuro *(adj.)*	dark, obscure
escaso *(adj.)*	scarce, thin, scanty
representante (m.n., f.n.)	representative
volar	to fly
vuelo	volamos
vuelas	voláis
vuela	vuelan
sacrificio *(m.n.)*	sacrifice
inferior *(adj.)*	lower, inferior
producción *(f.n.)*	production

pierna *(f.n.)*	leg
horizonte *(m.n.)*	horizon
remoto *(adj.)*	remote
nube *(f.n.)*	cloud
constitución *(f.n.)*	constitution
lenguaje *(m.n.)*	language
posibilidad *(f.n.)*	possibility
nervio *(m.n.)*	nerve
modesto *(adj.)*	modest
romanticismo *(m.n.)*	Romanticism
alzar	to raise (up), lift (up)
fijo *(adj.)*	fixed
bandera *(f.n.)*	flag, standard
esposa *(f.n.)*	wife
salud *(f.n.)*	health
poderoso *(adj.)*	powerful
imperio *(m.n.)*	empire
enterar	to inform, tell, pay
sindicato *(m.n.)*	trade union, syndicate
bosque *(m.n.)*	wood(land), forest

Unit 68

torno *(m.n.)*	bend, lathe, brake ('en torno a', 'round, about')
edición *(f.n.)*	edition, publishing
pintor (m.n., f.n.)	painter
salón *(m.n.)*	drawing-room, lounge, parlour
preocupar	to preoccupy
institución *(f.n.)*	institution
patio *(m.n.)*	patio, court(yard)
crisis *(f.n.)* (pl. las crisis)	crisis
estudiante (m.n., f.n.)	student
rodear	to surround, enclose, shut in
operación *(f.n.)*	operation
arquitectura *(f.n.)*	architecture
retirar	to move (away, back), withdraw, retire
idioma *(m.n.)*	language
seguridad *(f.n.)*	security
suya *(pron.)*	your(s), his, hers, its, their(s)
inmediatamente *(adv.)*	inmediately
director *(m.n.)* (f.n. directriz)	director, manager
inmediato *(adj.)*	immediate
durar	to last, survive, continue

americano *(adj.)*	American
crecer	to grow
crezco	crecemos
creces	crecéis
crece	crecen
vía *(f.n.)*	road, route, way, system
abuelo *(m.n.)*	grandfather
determinar	to determine, decide
izquierda *(f.n.)*	left(hand)(side)
prisa *(f.n.)*	hurry, haste
mientras *(conj.)*	while, as long as
cansar	to tire, fatigue (cansarse, to get tired)
técnico *(adj.)*	technical
sereno *(adj.)*	serene, peaceful
viuda *(f.n.)*	widow
árabe *(adj.)*	Arab(ic)
comparar	to compare
diario *(m.n.)*	newspaper, diary
misterioso *(adj.)*	mysterious
primitivo *(adj.)*	primitive
dividir	to divide
constar	to be clear, available, known
todos *(pron.)*	all, everything

conducta *(f.n.)*	conduct, management
siquiera *(adv.)*	at least (ni siquiera, not even)
aguardar	to (a)wait, expect
traducir	to translate
traduzco	traducimos
traduces	traducís
traduce	traducen
encanto *(m.n.)*	charm, enchantment
mejor *(m.n.)*	the better, the best
hierro *(m.n.)*	iron
drama *(m.n.)*	drama
admitir	to admit
carretera *(f.n.)*	road, highway
visible *(adj.)*	visible
buque *(m.n.)*	ship
soñar	to dream
diputado *(m.n.)*	representative, deputy
ingeniero *(m.n.)*	engineer
primavera *(f.n.)*	Spring
claridad *(f.n.)*	brightness, clarity
futuro *(adj.)*	future
largo *(m.n.)*	length
declaración *(f.n.)*	declaration

directament *(adv.)*	directly
colonia *(f.n.)*	colony
organismo *(m.n.)*	organization, organism
corriente *(adj.)*	running, normal, current
¡adiós! (interj.)	goodbye!
defecto *(m.n.)*	defect
tristeza *(f.n.)*	sadness
doble *(adj.)*	double
cuarenta *(num.)*	forty
principalmente *(adv.)*	principally
longitud (f.b.)	length, longitude
empresa *(f.n.)*	enterprise
gobernador *(m.n.)*	governor
criado *(m.n.)*	man(servant)
peor *(adj.)*	worse, worst
nombrar	to name, designate
enamorado *(adj.)*	in love
vecino *(m.n.)*	neighbour
documento *(m.n.)*	document
fascismo *(m.n.)*	fascism

dorado *(adj.)*	golden, gilt
extranjero *(m.n.)*	foreign lang(s), alien
apertura *(f.n.)*	opening
inútil *(adj.)*	useless
precisar	to need, specify
cura *(m.n.) (f.n.)*	priest, remedy
capa *(f.n.)*	cape, clock, layer
alejar	to move away, remove
ministerio *(m.n.)*	ministry
vestir	to dress, wear
visto	vestimos
vistes	vestís
viste	visten
beso *(m.n.)*	kiss
segundo *(m.n.)*	second
cárcel *(f.n.)*	prison
total *(adj.)*	total
elevado *(adj.)*	high, exalted
atribuir	to atribute
atribuyo	atribuimos
atribuyes	atribuís
atribuye	atribuyen
cesar	to stop, dismiss
facilitar	to facilitate
individual *(adj.)*	individual
definitivo *(adj.)*	definitive, final

imaginación *(f.n.)*	imagination
periodista (m.n., f.n.)	journalist
simpatía *(f.n.)*	liking, affection, charm
contribuir	to contribute
contribuyo	contribuimos
contribuyes	contribuís
contribuye	contribuyen
abajo *(adv.)*	down(wards), (stairs), under(neath)
progreso *(m.n.)*	progress
encender	to light, switch on
enciendo	encendemos
enciendes	encendéis
enciende	encienden
indispensable *(adj.)*	indispensable
menos *(adj.)*	less, fewer, minus
muerto *(m.n.)*	dead person, corpse
descansar	to rest
afirmación *(f.n.)*	affirmation
punto *(f.n.)*	point, end, tip
rojo *(m.n.)*	red (colour)
foco *(m.n.)*	focus, spotlight
oponer	to oppose
opongo	oponemos
opones	oponéis
opone	oponen
primero *(m.n.)*	first (thing)
sospechar	to suspect
únicamente *(adj.)*	solely, uniquely
reacción *(f.n.)*	reaction

desgracia *(f.n.)*	misfortune, accident
actuar	to work, operate, function
actúo	actuamos
actúas	actuáis
actúa	actúan
lástima *(f.n.)*	shame, pity
influir	to influence
influyo	influimos
influyes	influís
influye	influyen
ropa *(f.n.)*	clothes
quejarse	to complain
violento *(adj.)*	violent
adoptar	to adopt
discípulo *(m.n.)*	disciple, pupil
taller *(m.n.)*	workshop, factory
quinto *(adj.)*	fifth
gana *(f.n.)*	desire, wish
misión *(f.n.)*	mission
opuesto *(adj.)*	opposed
amoroso *(adj.)*	loving, affectionate
relativo *(adj.)*	relative
dedo *(m.n.)*	finger, toe
proporcionar	to suppy, provide, lend
colegio *(m.n.)*	school, college
bien *(m.n.)*	advantage, good

kilómetro *(m.n.)*	kilometre
paseo *(m.n.)*	stroll, outing
cifra *(f.n.)*	number
insistir	to insist
creencia *(f.n.)*	belief
obispo *(m.n.)*	bishop
despacho *(m.n.)*	dispatch, office, promptness
prometer	to promise
tardar	to delay, be long, be late
policía *(f.n.)(m.n.)*	police (force), policeman (policía femenino, policewoman)
reina *(f.n.)*	queen
amiga *(f.n.)*	(girl-)friend, lover
reducido *(adj.)*	reduced
hombro *(m.n.)*	shoulder
respuesta *(f.n.)*	answer
ideal *(adj.)*	ideal
soledad *(f.n.)*	solitude, loneliness
clima *(m.n.)*	climate
abuela *(f.n.)*	grandmother, old lady
economía *(f.n.)*	economy, economics

Unit 76

oriental *(adj.)*	eastern, oriental
aparte *(adv.)*	separately, aside
portugués *(adj.)*	Portugese
desnudo *(adj.)*	bare, naked
información *(f.n.)*	information
latín *(adj.)*	Latin
veinticinco *(num.)*	twenty-five
automóvil *(m.n.)*	car
lógico *(adj.)*	logical
mente *(f.n.)*	mind
aldea *(f.n.)*	village
mía *(pron.)*	mine (f.)
conquista *(f.n.)*	conquest
infinito *(adj.)*	infinite
lluvia *(f.n.)*	rain(fall), shower
revolucionar	to rouse to revolt, revolutionize
variedad *(f.n.)*	variety
período *(m.n.)*	period
norma *(f.n.)*	norm
azul *(m.n.)*	blue (colour)

crítico *(adj.)*	critical
por tanto *(conj.)*	so, therefore
temblar	to tremble, shake
virgen *(f.n.)*	virgin
divertir	to amuse, distract
divierto	divertimos
diviertes	divertís
divierte	divierten
juez (m.n., f.n.) (also f. jueza)	judge
inventar	to invent
locura *(f.n.)*	madness
verdaderamente *(adv.)*	really, truly
recién *(adv.)*	just, recently
odio *(m.n.)*	hatred
asustar	to frighten
decisivo *(adj.)*	decisive
reúnion *(f.n.)*	reunion
gasto *(m.n.)*	expense, wear, waste
llave *(f.n.)*	key
adivinar	to foretell, solve
decreto *(m.n.)*	decree
pintura *(f.n.)*	painting
perdido *(adj.)*	lost

Unit 78

chica *(f.n.)*	girl, maid(servant)
nacida *(adj.)*	born
regresar	to return, give back, send back
atacar	to attack
catedral *(f.n.)*	cathedral
formidable *(adj.)*	terrific, redoubtable
aspirar	to breathe in, aspire
ruido *(m.n.)*	noise, commotion, sound
calor *(m.n.)*	heat, warmth
emprender	to underake, attack
seguido *(adj.)*	straight, continuous
caminar	to walk, travel
exclusivamente *(adv.)*	exclusively
tranquilidad *(f.n.)*	calmness
preparado *(adj.)*	prepared
confirmar	to confirm
atrás *(adv.)*	back, behind
final *(m.n.) (f.n.)*	ending, final (sport)
tratado *(m.n.)*	treaty, agreement
presente *(m.n.)*	present

hospital *(m.n.)*	hospital
militar *(m.n.)*	soldier
sexual *(adj.)*	sexual
barrio *(m.n.)*	suburb, district
salida *(f.n.)*	exit, departure
cobre *(m.n.)*	copper
loco *(m.n.)*	lunatic
encargar	to entrust, order, change
recorrer	to travel, go over, cross
unión *(f.n.)*	union
considerado *(adj.)*	considered
respetar	to respect
formación *(f.n.)*	formation
vieja *(f.n.)*	old woman
humilde *(adj.)*	humble
risa *(f.n.)*	laugh(ter)
independiente *(adj.)*	independent
silencioso *(adj.)*	silent
agudo *(adj.)*	sharp, acute
comentar	to comment

máquina *(f.n.)*	machine(ry), engine, camera, car
profesional *(adj.)*	professional
saltar	to jump (over), spring, fly up
afán *(m.n.)*	desire, anxiety, toil
colección *(f.n.)*	collection
hueso *(m.n.)*	bone
matiz *(m.n.)*	shade
heroico *(adj.)*	heroic
quemar	to burn
revelar	to reveal
simpático *(adj.)*	likeable, nice
auténtico *(f.n.)*	genuine
composición *(f.n.)*	composition
hipótesis *(f.n.)* (pl. hipótesis)	hypothesis
paralelo *(adj.)*	parallel
sentado *(adj.)*	seated, sensible
sombrero *(m.n.)*	hat
dictadura *(f.n.)*	dictatorship
ninguno *(pron.)*	nobody, neither
extenso *(adj.)*	extensive

instrucción *(f.n.)*	instruction, knowledge, training
escrito *(m.n.)*	document, writing, brief
integral *(adj.)*	complete, integral
prolongación *(f.n.)*	extensión
miseria *(f.n.)*	poverty, squalor
situado *(adj.)*	situated
sal *(f.n.)*	salt
citado *(adj.)*	aforementioned
apellido *(m.n.)*	family name, surname
contrario *(adj.)*	opposite, contrary
manuscrito *(m.n.)*	manuscript
católico *(adj.)*	Catholic
notable *(adj.)*	notable
lujo *(m.n.)*	luxury
daño *(m.n.)*	damage, injury
práctica *(f.n.)*	practice
serenidad *(f.n.)*	serenity
vino *(m.n.)*	wine
rechazar	to throw back, repel, push away
átome *(m.n.)*	atom

formado *(adj.)*	formed
mercado *(m.n.)*	market
comentario *(m.n.)*	commentary
trágico *(adj.)*	tragic
cultivar	to grow, cultivate
besar	to kiss
tragedia *(f.n.)*	tragedy
mueble *(m.n.)*	piece of furniture (muebles, furniture)
correspondiente *(adj.)*	corresponding
rogar	to beg (for), plead
ruego	rogamos
ruegas	rogáis
ruega	ruegan
ventaja *(f.n.)*	advantage
aplicar	to apply, impose, assign
confundir	to confuse, confound, lose
descender	to drop, lower, take down, descend
desciendo	descendemos
desciendes	descendéis
desciende	descienden
hallazgo *(m.n.)*	find(ing), discovery
cualidad *(f.n.)*	quality
molino *(m.n.)*	mill
sierra *(f.n.)*	mountain-range, saw
ajeno *(adj.)*	outside, foreign, belonging to someone else
cristiano *(adj.)*	Christian

mentir	to lie
miento	mentimos
mientes	mentís
miente	mienten
poético *(adj.)*	poetic
utilizar	to use
concesión *(f.n.)*	concession
instituto *(m.n.)*	institute, school
cueva *(f.n.)*	cave
enamorar	to win love, inspire love (enamorarse, to fall in love)
consentir	to allow, admit, agree
consiento	consentimos
consientes	consentís
consiente	consienten
suficiente *(adj.)*	sufficient
desconocido *(adj.)*	unknown
víctima *(f.n.)*	victim
decidido *(adj.)*	resolute, determined
junio *(f.n.)*	June
local *(adj.)*	local
equivocar	to mistake (equivocarse, to be wrong)
disminuir	to decrease
explicación *(f.n.)*	explanation
disciplina *(f.n.)*	discipline
silla *(f.n.)*	chair
generoso *(adj.)*	generous

Unit 84

pájara *(m.n.)*	bird
interior *(m.n.)*	interior
espectro *(m.n.)*	spectrum, spectre
singular *(adj.)*	singular
calidad *(f.n.)*	quality
fresco *(adj.)*	cool, fresh
poema *(m.n.)*	poem
viajar	to travel
madrileño *(adj.)*	of Madrid
embajador *(m.n.)*	ambassador
infierno *(m.n.)*	hell
rápidamente *(adv.)*	quickly
temperamento *(m.n.)*	temperament
estrecho *(adj.)*	narrow, tight, strict
lágrima *(f.n.)*	tear
nacimiento *(m.n.)*	birth
posterior *(adj.)*	later, back, rear
estético *(adj.)*	aesthetic
banco *(m.n.)*	bank, bench
supremo *(adj.)*	supreme

invierno *(m.n.)*	winter
millar *(m.n.)*	thousand
aconsejar	to advise
estimar	to esteem, estimate
solitario *(adj.)*	lonely, solitary
pasaje *(m.n.)*	passage(way), passing
luchar	to struggle, wrestle
orgullo *(m.n.)*	pride
delicioso *(adj.)*	delicious
amante (m.n., f.n.)	lover
percibir	to perceive, earn
someter	to conquer, submit
firme *(adj.)*	firm, steady
mando *(m.n.)*	command, lead
titulado *(adj.)*	(en)titled
ala *(f.n.)*	wing
glorioso *(adj.)*	glorious
librar	to save, free, deliver
octubre *(m.n.)*	October
indio *(m.n.)*	Indian

angustia *(f.n.)*	anguish, distress
reloj *(m.n.)*	clock, watch
humor *(m.n.)*	humour (U.S. humor)
pobreza *(f.n.)*	poverty
superar	to overcome, excel
municipal *(adj.)*	municipal
vecino *(adj.)*	neighbouring, near(by)
alegrar	to cheer (up) (alegrarse, to be delighted)
tarea *(f.n.)*	job, task
pareja *(f.n.)*	pair, couple
evidente *(adj.)*	evident
sujeto *(m.n.)*	subject
¡bah! (interj.)	bah! Never!
castellano *(adj.)*	Castilian (by extension, Spanish)
rasgo *(m.n.)*	stroke, gesture (pl. features, characteristics)
temor *(m.n.)*	fear
alcalde *(m.n.)*	mayor
cuarto *(adj.)*	fourth
disparar	to shoot
proporción *(f.n.)*	proportion

delicado *(adj.)*	delicate, dainty, choosy
avisar	to inform, tell, warn
batalla *(f.n.)*	battle
substituir	to substitute
substituyo	substituimos
substituyes	substituís
substituye	substituyen
vulgar *(adj.)*	ordinary, vulgar
estancia *(f.n.)*	ranch, farm, stay, dwelling
disco *(m.n.)*	disc(us), disco(theque)
carecer	to lack
carezco	carecemos
careces	carecéis
carece	carecen
evolución *(f.n.)*	evolution
ayuntamiento *(m.n.)*	town or city council, town or city hall
metro *(m.n.)*	metre, underground
sabio *(adj.)*	wise, sensible
variar	to vary
varío	variamos
varías	variáis
varía	varían
actualidad *(f.n.)*	present (time) (pl. actualidades, current events)
ceder	to yield, give away, hand over
cuello *(m.n.)*	neck
impulso *(m.n.)*	impulse
convicción *(f.n.)*	conviction
femenino *(adj.)*	feminine
noventa *(num.)*	ninety

Unit 88

desconocer	disavow
desconozco	desconocemos
desconoces	desconocéis
desconoce	desconocen
franco *(adj.)*	frank, free, clear
crónica *(f.n.)*	chronicle, feature
lento *(adj.)*	slow
sonrisa *(f.n.)*	smile
julio *(m.n.)*	July
plazo *(m.n.)*	period, deadline, instalment
sesenta *(num.)*	sixty
arreglar	to arrange, settle
típico *(adj.)*	typical
alcoba *(f.n.)*	bedroom
mental *(adj.)*	mental
permanente *(adj.)*	permanent
admirar	to admire, surprise
inteligente *(adj.)*	intelligent
miembro *(m.n.)*	member, limb
pasear	to stroll, walk (about)
radio *(f.n.)*	radio
apoyar	to learn, rest, support
conveniente *(adj.)*	convenient

rincón *(m.n.)*	corner
célebre *(adj.)*	famous
arroz *(m.n.)*	rice
griego *(m.n.)*	Greek (language, person)
absurdo *(adj.)*	absurd
¡hola! (interj.)	hullo!
contento *(adj.)*	happy, satisfied
merced *(f.n.)*	favour, reward
paraíso *(m.n.)*	paradise
red *(f.n.)*	net(work)
fácilmente *(adv.)*	easily
deuda *(f.n.)*	debt
bailar	to dance
sexto *(adj.)*	sixth
agradable *(adj.)*	agreeable
ciudadano *(m.n.)*	citizen
mecanismo *(m.n.)*	machinery, mechanism
oriente *(m.n.)*	east, orient
prosa *(f.n.)*	prose
enfermo *(adj.)*	sick

Unit 90

inspirar	to inspire
comunicación *(f.n.)*	communication
excepción *(f.n.)*	exception
firmar	to sign
orientación *(f.n.)*	orientation
colectivo *(adj.)*	collective
definitivamente *(adv.)*	finally
fiel *(adj.)*	faithful
manejo *(m.n.)*	management, confidence, intrigue
programa *(m.n.)*	programme (U.S. program)
acompañado *(adj.)*	accompanied
cadáver *(m.n.)*	corpse
expresivo *(adj.)*	expressive
ladrón *(m.n.)*	thief
órgano *(m.n.)*	organ
medir	to measure
mido	medimos
mides	medís
mide	miden
orilla *(f.n.)*	edge, shore
conclusión *(f.n.)*	conclusion
modo *(f.n.)*	fashion
pintado *(adj.)*	spotted, colourful

nuestro *(pron.)*	ours, of ours
ataque *(m.n.)*	attack
renunciar	to renounce, resign
examen *(m.n.)*	examination
incluir	to include
incluyo	incluimos
incluyes	incluís
incluye	incluyen
siguiera *(conj.)*	even if, even though
agosto *(m.n.)*	August
decisión *(f.n.)*	decision
requerir	to require, send for
requiero	requerimos
requieres	requerís
requiere	requieren
sentimental *(adj.)*	sentimental
ciego *(adj.)*	blind
espléndido *(adj.)*	splendid
peso *(m.n.)*	weight, unit of currency of some Latin American countries
combinación *(f.n.)*	combination, connection, scheme
fraile *(m.n.)*	friar
renacimiento *(m.n.)*	renaissance
terminado *(m.n.)*	ended, finished
aislado *(adj.)*	isolated
descuidar	to neglect, disregard
parlamento *(m.n.)*	parliament

Unit 92

gas *(m.n.)*	gas
resistencia *(f.n.)*	resistance
invisible *(adj.)*	invisible
sensibilidad *(f.n.)*	sensibility
llover	to rain
llueve	rains
vergüenza *(f.n.)*	shame
séptimo *(adj.)*	seventh
útil *(adj.)*	useful
resumen *(m.n.)*	summary
ayuda *(f.n.)*	aid
mediterráneo *(adj.)*	Mediterranean
casino *(m.n.)*	club, casino
combate *(m.n.)*	battle, fight
químico *(adj.)*	chemical
mancha *(f.n.)*	mark, stain
extrañar	to wonder at, deport
continuo *(adj.)*	continuous, continual
cuartel *(m.n.)*	quarter, barracks
establecido *(adj.)*	established
occidental *(adj.)*	western

tontería *(f.n.)*	foolishness
cordial *(adj.)*	friendly
meditar	to meditate, think (over)
gastar	to spend, waste, wear away
débil *(adj.)*	wear
intervención *(f.n.)*	intervention
último *(m.n.)*	(the) last
cruz *(f.n.)*	cross
ansia *(f.n.)*	anxiety, longing
oposición *(f.n.)*	opposition
demonio *(m.n.)*	devil
bolsillo *(m.n.)*	pocker(book), purse
egoísmo *(m.n.)*	egotism
capacidad *(f.n.)*	capacity
distraer	to distract, amuse, relax
distraigo	distraemos
distraes	distraéis
distrae	distraen
tesoro *(m.n.)*	treasure, treasury
pastor *(m.n.)*	shepherd, clergyman
reforma *(f.n.)*	reform(ation), (pl. repairs)
socialista *(adj.)*	socialist
acertar	to manage, get it right

grandeza *(f.n.)*	greatness, size, grandeur
intenso *(adj.)*	intense
oler	to smell (out)
huelo	olemos
hueles	oléis
huele	huelen
político *(m.n.)*	political
amenazar	to threaten
redondo *(adj.)*	round
caja *(f.n.)*	cash(box), cashier's office, box, case
maldito *(adj.)*	damned
polvo *(m.n.)*	dust, powder
ruina *(f.n.)*	ruin
antigüedad *(f.n.)*	age, antique, antiquity
párrafo *(m.n.)*	paragraph
sincero *(adj.)*	sincere
campaña *(f.n.)*	countryside, campaign
asociación *(f.n.)*	association
llegada *(f.n.)*	arrival
diario *(adj.)*	daily
intervenir	to intervene
intervengo	intervenimos
intervienes	intervenís
interviene	intervienen
dueño *(m.n.)*	master, owner, employer
moral *(f.n.)*	morals, morality

justificar	to justify
claro *(adv.)*	clearly
llegado *(adj.)*	arrived
abril *(m.n.)*	April
temporada *(f.n.)*	season, period
chino *(m.n.)*	Chinese
presidencia *(f.n.)*	presidency
recurso *(m.n.)*	recourse, means (pl. resources)
frío *(m.n.)*	cold
dibujo *(m.n.)*	drawing, design
castige *(m.n.)*	punishment
traducción *(f.n.)*	translation
veintiséis *(num.)*	twenty-six
anciono *(m.n.)*	elderly man
baño *(m.n.)*	bath(ing), toilet
enemigo *(adj.)*	enemy
pegar	to hit, strike, stick (on)
voto *(m.n.)*	vote, vow
devolver	to hand back, return
devuelvo	devolvemos
devuelves	devolvéis
devuelve	devuelven
testimonio *(m.n.)*	evidence

Unit 96

dignidad *(f.n.)*	dignity, rank
honrado *(adj.)*	honourable, honest
premio *(m.n.)*	prize
muchedumbre *(f.n.)*	crowd, mob
esposo *(m.n.)*	husband
coronel *(m.n.)*	colonel
dominio *(m.n.)*	domain, dominion
apagar	to put out, switch off
indudable *(adj.)*	undoubted
victoria *(f.n.)*	victory
canción *(f.n.)*	song
prólogo *(m.n.)*	prologue
sorpresa *(f.n.)*	surprise
novia *(f.n.)*	fiancée, bride
empeño *(m.n.)*	determination
expuesto *(adj.)*	exposed, displayed
cocina *(f.n.)*	cookery, cooker, kitchen
integrar	to comprise
violencia *(f.n.)*	violence
curar	to cure, recover

futuro *(m.n.)*	future
concluir	to conclude
concluyo	concluimos
concluyes	concluís
concluye	concluyen
esfera *(f.n.)*	sphere, globe
moro *(m.n.)*	Moor
busca *(f.n.)*	search, (but m.n. bleeping device)
obligación *(f.n.)*	obligation, bond
cenar	to dine
educación *(f.n.)*	education
pálido *(adj.)*	pale
destacar	to emphasize, bring out, detach
rendir	to produce, conquer
rindo	rendimos
rindes	rendís
rinde	rinden
positivo *(adj.)*	positive
elección *(f.n.)*	election
exterior *(adj.)*	external, exterior
cansancio *(m.n.)*	fatigue
decoración *(f.n.)*	decoration
presupuesto *(m.n.)*	budget, estimate
seda *(f.n.)*	silk
escaleral *(f.n.)*	steps, staircase
final *(adj.)*	final

galán *(m.n.)*	handsome man, suitor, male lead
rebelde *(adj.)*	rebellious
prescindir	to omit, dispense with
oportuno *(adj.)*	timely, suitable
constantemente *(adv.)*	constantly
cuerda *(f.n.)*	rope, string, energy
escándalo *(m.n.)*	scandal
pureza *(f.n.)*	purity
transformar	to transform
episodio *(m.n.)*	episode
castillo *(m.n.)*	castle
acontecimiento *(m.n.)*	event
concurrir	to agree, meet, contribute
diecisiete *(m.n.)*	seventeen
elegir	to elect
elijo	elegimos
eliges	elegís
elige	eligen
invitar	to invite
material *(adj.)*	material, physical
probablemente *(adv.)*	probably
tradicional *(adj.)*	traditional
diecinueve *(num.)*	ninteen

amarillo *(adj.)*	yellow
veinticuatro *(num.)*	twenty-four
admiración *(f.n.)*	admiration
multitud *(f.n.)*	multitude
otoño *(m.n.)*	Autumn
grato *(adj.)*	pleasant
jornada *(f.n.)*	hours of work, day's journey
empleado *(m.n.)*	employé
normal *(adj.)*	normal
copiar	to copy
sillón *(m.n.)*	armchair
aludir	to mention
juntar	to join, collect
caracterizar	to characterize
consideración *(f.n.)*	consideration
obligado *(adj.)*	obliged
verde *(m.n.)*	green (colour)
liberalismo *(m.n.)*	liberalism
indefinible *(adj.)*	indefinable
cliente (m.n., f.n.)	client

mayo *(m.n.)*	May
diablo *(m.n.)*	devil
dieciocho *(num.)*	eighteen
tertulia *(f.n.)*	gathering
eficaz *(adj.)*	efficient, effective
democrático *(adj.)*	democratic
introducir	to introduce
introduzco	introducimos
introduces	introducís
introduce	introducen
trato *(m.n.)*	relations(hip), treatment
alumno *(m.n.)*	pupil
culto *(m.n.)*	cult, worship
beneficio *(m.n.)*	benefit, profit, exploitation
marcar	to mark (off, out), score
oficina *(f.n.)*	office, workshop
robar	to rob
empujar	to push
horror *(m.n.)*	horror
sucesión *(f.n.)*	succession
acusar	to show, denounce, reveal
destruir	to destroy
destruyo	destruimos
destruyes	destruís
destruye	destruyen
infantil *(adj.)*	children's

INDEXES

muchacha 32
muchacho 45
muchedumbre 96
mucho 5, 9, 47
mueble 82
muerte 19
muerto 49, 73
mujer 4
multitud 99
mundo 6
municipal 86
muro 58
museo 60
música 56

nacer 20
nacido 78
nacimiento 84
nación 29
nacional 19
nada 8, 10, 64
nadie 9
natural 17
naturaleza 31
naturalmente 47
necesario 26
necesidad 28
necesitar 15
negar 38
negocio 48
negro 21
nervio 67
nervioso 33
ni 4
ninguno 10, 80
niña 26
niño 14
no 1
noble 54
noche 8
nombrar 71
nombre 9
norma 76
normal 99
norte 31
nota 36
notable 81
notar 34
noticia 17

novedad 64
novela 14
novelista 53
noventa 87
novia 96
novio 50
nube 67
nuestro 3, 91
nueve 13
nuevo 6, 45
número 13
numeroso 35
nunca 8

o 2
obispo 75
objetivo 34
objeto 16
obligación 97
obligado 99
obligar 44
obra 6
obrero 31
observación 34
observar 27
obtener 34
ocasión 23
occidental 92
octavo 41
octubre, 85
ocultar 59
ocupar 19
ocurrir 15
ochenta 39
ocho 12
odio 77
oficial 48
oficina 100
oficio 58
ofrecer 17
¡oh! 39
oír 7
ojo 8
oler 94
olvidar 19
once 65
operación 68
opinión 24
oponer 73

oportuno 98
oposición 93
opuesto 74
organismo 71
organización 38
organizar 59
órgano 90
orgullo 85
orientación 90
oriental 76
oriente 89
origen 21
original 63
orilla 90
oro 23
oscuro 66
otoño 99
otro 2, 10

padre 8
pagar 29
página 30
país 10
paisaje 62
pájaro 84
palabra 8
palacio 35
pálido 97
pan 51
papá 61
papel 21
par 64
para 2
paraíso 89
paralelo 80
parar 56
parecer 5
pared 44
pareja 86
parlamento 91
párrafo 94
parte 5
particular 40
partido 21
partir 38
pasado 27, 52
pasaje 85
pasar 4
pasear 88

seguro 34
seis 11
semana 36
semejante 57
sencillo 56
sensación 51
sensibilidad 92
sentado 80
sentar 23
sentido 14
sentimental 91
sentimiento 22
sentir 8
señalar 37
señor 4
señora 7
señorita 24
señorito 57
separar 55
séptimo 92
ser 1, 31
serenidad 81
sereno 69
serie 26
serio 53
servicio 24
servir 10
sesenta 88
setenta 61
sexto 89
sexual 79
si 2
sí 4
siempre 5
sierra 82
siete 18
siglo 8
significar 33
siguiente 16
silencio 32
silencioso 79
silla 83
sillón 99
simpatía 73
simpático 80
simple 34
sin 3
sincero 94
sindicato 67

singular 84
sino 6
siguiera 70, 91
sistema 27
sitio 40
situación 26
situado 81
sobre 3
social 18
socialista 54, 93
sociedad 23
sol 18
solamente 45
soldado 55
soledad 75
soler 18
solitario 85
solo 11
sólo 5
solución 39
sombrero 80
someter 85
sonar 48
sonreír 63
sonrisa 88
soñar 70
sorprender 55
sorpresa 96
sospechar 73
sostener 39
su 1
suave 50
subir 27
substancia 48
substituir 87
suceder 25
sucesión 100
suceso 50
suelo 20
sueño 36
suerte 33
suficiente 83
sufrir 25
sujeto 86
superar 86
superficie 49
superior 32
suponer 21
supremo 84

sur 61
surgir 47
suya 68
suyo 61

tabla 50
tal 7
talento 61
taller 74
también 4
tan 4
tanto 9, 15
tardar 75
tarde 12, 37
tarea 86
teatro 25
técnica 33
técnico 69
televisión 24
tema 35
temblar 77
temer 48
temor 86
temperamento 84
temporada 95
tendencia 56
tender 56
tener 1
teoría 30
tercero 27
terminado 91
terminar 23
término 22
terreno 52
terrible 49
territorio 58
tertulia 100
tesoro 93
testimonio 95
texto 34
tía 41
tiempo 5
tierra 9
tío 59
típico 88
tipo 14
tirar 48
titulado 85
título 35

tocar 23
todavía 13
todo 2, 4
todos 69
tomar 9
tono 65
tontería 93
torno 68
toro 33
torre 61
total 72
trabajar 20
trabajo 9
tradición 42
tradicional 98
traducción 95
traducir 70
traer 12
tragedia 82
trágico 82
traje 54
tranquilidad 78
tranquilo 49
transformar 98
tras 63
trasladar 57
tratado 78
tratar 11
trato 100
través 37
treinta 21
tren 46
tres 5
triste 25
tristeza 71
triunfo 66
tropa 62
tu 7
tú 2

último 8, 93
un 1
una 1, 26
únicamente 73
única 17
unidad 52
unido 47
unión 79
unir 55

universal 54
universidad 21
uno 4, 9
usar 56
uso 38
usted 2
útil 92
utilizar 83

valer 23
valor 15
valle 26
variar 87
variedad 76
vario 13
vaso 14
vecino 71, 86
veinte 29
veinticinco 70
veintiséis 95
vencer 64
vender 35
venir 4
ventaja 82
ventana 30
ver 3
vera 61
verano 47
verde 43, 99
verdad 7
verdaderamente 77
verdadero 17
vergüenza 92
verso 41
vestido 52
vestir 72
vez 3
vía 69
viajar 84
viaje 21
viajero 54
víctima 83
victoria 96
vida 3
vídeo 62
vieja 79
viejo 14, 55
viento 56
villa 52

vino 81
violencia 96
violento 74
virgen 77
virtud 62
visible 70
visión 41
visita 50
visitar 31
vital 40
viuda 69
vivir 6
vivo 33
volar 66
volumen 64
voluntad 32
volver 6
voto 95
voz 18
vuelta 52
vuestro 45
vulgar 87

y 1
ya 2
yo 1

zona 22

local 83
lock (in) 59
lock up 59
logical 76
loneliness 75
lonely 85
long 16
long, be 75
longing 93
longitude 71
look 33
look at 7
lose 10, 82
lost 77
lot 47
lot of 5
lounge 68
love 10, 40
love, in 71
love, inspire 83
love, win 83
lover 75, 85
loving 74
low 38, 52
lower 31, 66, 82
luck 33
lunatic 79
luxury 81

machine(ry) 80, 89
mad 47
madness 77
Madrid 84
magnificent 43
maid(servant) 78
maintain 32
major 9
majority 42
make 2
male lead 98
man 3
man, elderly 95
man, handsome 98
manage 28, 32, 40, 93
management 70, 90
manager 68
manner 17
manufacture 66

manuscript 81
many 9
march 19, 62
marchioness 54
mark 36, 37, 92
mark off, out 100
market 82
marriage 39, 59
married couple 39
mass 32
master 17, 50, 94
match 21
mate 36
material 45, 98
materials 57
mathematical 50
mathematics 45
matter 23, 28, 45
May 100
mayor 86
meal 61
mean 33
meaning 14
meanwhile 20
measure(ment) 40, 90
meat 41
mechanism 89
medicine 53
Mediterranean 92
meditate 93
medium 17
meet 6, 98
meeting 43
member 88
memory 30, 34
mental 88
mention 63, 99
mentioned, above 13
merit 57
merry 43
metal 55
method 9, 22
metre 87
middle 17, 51
military 35
mill 82
million 32
mind 52, 65, 76
mine 53, 76

minister 20
ministry 72
minor 36
minus 73
minute 27
mirror 48
misfortune 58, 74
mislead 49
miss 24
mission 74
mistake 83
Mr 4
Mrs 7, 16
mob 96
model 49
modern 22
modest 67
mom 55
moment 8
monastery 41
money 19, 45
month 13
Moor 97
moral 46
morality 94
morals 94
more 2
moreover 14
morning 11
mother 10
motive 22
mountain 45, 60
mountain-range 82
mouth 27
move 35, 57
move away 68, 72
move back 68
movement 22
much 5, 9, 15
multitude 99
mummy 55
municipal 86
museum 60
music 56
my 2
myself 23
mysterious 69
mystery 59

station 30
stay 87
steady 29, 85
step 19, 34
steps 97
stick (on) 95
still 13
stone 26
step 23, 56, 72
storey 42, 65
story 38
straight 21, 78
strange 32
street 9
strength 11
stretch (out) 56
strict 84
strike 95
string 98
stroke 86
stroll 75, 88
strong 34
structure 47
struggle 37, 85
student 68
study 11, 18
style 47
subject 28, 86
submit 85
substance 48
substitute 87
suburb 79
succeed 25
success 54
succession 100
such 7
suffer 25, 62
suffice 24
sufficient 39, 83
sufficiently 59
suit 54
suitable 98
suitor 98
sum(mary) 41, 92
summer 47
sun 18
Sunday 53
superior 32
supply 74

support 88
suppose 21
supreme 84
sure 34
surely 53
surface 49
surname 81
surprise 55, 88, 96
surround 68
survive 68
suspect 73
sustain 39
swear 43
sweet 41
sweetheart 50
switch off 96
switch on 73
syndicate 67
system 27, 69

table 27, 50
take 57
take away 29
take down 82
take hold of 43
take off 29
talent 61
tall 12
task 86
taste 22
teach 36
teacher 17, 46
teaching 65
tear 84
tear away 51
tear off 51
technical 69
technique 33
technology 33
television 24
tell 10, 67, 87
temperament 84
ten 23
tend 56
tendency 56
tenth 9
term 22
terrible 49

terrific 78
territory 58
test 33, 61
text 34
thank 61
that 1, 3, 10, 23, 34, 57, 65
the 1
theatre 28
than 1, 68
theirs 61, 68
theme 65
then 4, 8, 9
theory 36
there 12, 16, 23
therefore 77
they 2
thick 57
thief 90
thin 66
thing 5
think 6
think (over) 93
third 27
thirty 21
this 2, 5, 7, 11
though 9
thought 18
thousand 85
threaten 94
three 5
through I
throw (away) 48
throw (back) 81
thrown (down, out, up) 51
thus 5
tight 84
time 3, 5
timely 98
tip 73
tare 69
title 35
to 1, 2
today 7
toe 74
together 44, 54
together, get 43
toil 80

toilet 95
tomorrow 11, 54
tone 65
tongue 45
too 4, 39
too (much) 51
top, on 35
total 72
touch 23
towards 11
tower 61
town 52
town council 87
town hall 87
trade 58
trade union 67
tradition 42
traditional 98
tragedy 82
tragic 82
train 36, 46
training 81
transfer 57
transform 98
translate 57, 70
translation 95
travel 78, 79, 84
traveller 54
treasure 93
treasury 93
treatment 100
treaty 78
tree 30
tremble 77
trial 62
trip 21, 62
triumph 56
troop 62
trouble 47
true 17
truly 77
trust 64
truth 7
truthful 17
try 29, 40, 61
turn 52
twelve 50
twenty 29
twenty-five 76

twenty-four 99
twenty-six 95
two 3
type 14
typical 88

uncle 59
under 53, 73
underground 87
underneath 53, 73
understand 14, 19
undertake 78
undoubted 96
unfold 56
union 79
unique 17
uniquely 73
unit 52
unite 55
united 47
unity 52
universal 54
university 21
unknown 83
unpleasant 13
until 4
up 62
upper 32
use 29, 38, 56, 58, 83
useful 92
useless 72

valley 26
value 15
variable 13
varied 13
variety 76
vary 87
verse 4 1
very 3
victim 83
victory 96
video (recorder) 62
villa 52
village 6, 75
violence 96
violent 74

virgin 77
virtue 62
visible 70
vision 41
visit 31, 50
vital 40
voice 18
void 64
volume 64
vote 95
vow 95
vulgar 87

wake (up) 43
walk 19, 62, 78
walk about 88
wall 44, 58
want 3
war 12
warmth 78
warn 87
waste 77, 93
water 14
way 9, 11, 17, 36, 69
way, give 87
we 2
week 93
wealth 56
weapon 41
wear 72, 77
wear away 93
wearing 35
wedding 59
week 36
weep 24
weigh 26
weight 91
well 4, 5
western 92
what 1
whatever 46
when 3, 12
where 5, 57
whether 2
which 1, 6
which, of 15, 17
whichever 27
while 20, 37, 69

Also available in this series from Oleander:

Arabic Key Words   9780906672273
English Key Words   9780906672907
French Key Words   9780906672242
German Key Words   9780906672280
Greek Key Words (Classical Greek)   9780906672853
Italian Key Words   9780906672259
Latin Key Words   9780906672693

30287092R00081

Printed in Great Britain
by Amazon